Literature Review

AF800079

INVESTMENT PROFESSIONALS AND FIDUCIARY DUTIES

Marianne M. Jennings

CFA Institute Research Foundation

Statement of Purpose

The CFA Institute Research Foundation is a not-for-profit organization established to promote the development and dissemination of relevant research for investment practitioners worldwide.

ISBN 978-1-934667-75-0

17 September 2014

Editorial Staff

Ellen Barber
Editor

Cindy Maisannes
Manager, Publications Production

Randy Carila
Publishing Technology Specialist

Investment Professionals and Fiduciary Duties

Marianne M. Jennings
Professor Emeritus of Legal and Ethical Studies in Business
Arizona State University
Tempe, Arizona

> "How do we structure regulation so that it encourages best practices, . . . doesn't overly impact markets in ways that markets shouldn't be impacted and let[s] markets operate in ways that markets should be allowed to operate?"
>
> —Paul Roth[1]

Introduction

Whether a fiduciary standard should be applied to all of the various roles investment professionals play in the financial markets has been and continues to be the subject of legal, regulatory, and ethical debate (Gillis 1972; Gillis and Weld 1972). Analysts play diverse roles in the financial markets. Analysts who work on the sell side provide information about investment banking services that their employers provide to issuers. These employers appreciate any optimism their employee analysts can muster about clients' securities. Some sell-side analysts provide fairness opinions in mergers, another type of transaction in whose success the analysts' employers have an interest. Other analysts purchase and sell securities for individual clients. Still other analysts provide investment management services for large funds, including mutual and pension funds. In their work as fund managers, analysts also provide research in exchange for those soft dollars that were intended as a means of resolving conflicts of interest in research results. And there is inherent tension between financial market participants and professionals because of their different financial stakes. Clients want to maximize returns on their investments, employers want certain investment vehicles sold, professionals and their associations seek to earn trust and respect from both investors and the public, and markets seek stability and transparency.

The roles of investment professionals are diverse, but in all of these roles, there is a common thread of inherent conflict of interest (Droms 1992). As Walsh and Johns (2013) phrase it:

[1]"Symposium: The Regulation of Investment Funds," *Fordham Journal of Corporate & Finance Law*, vol. 16, no. 1 (2011), p. 63.

> The Biblical admonition that a person cannot serve two masters is at the heart of the problem in applying a fiduciary standard to a broker-dealers transaction-based commission business. By its very nature as a for-profit entity, a broker-dealer will inherently act in its own financial interest by dealing for its own account and by striving to maximize its profits. (p. 445)

Optimism is important to investment professionals' employers, their clients, other underwriters, and markets. Less optimism means fewer investors. Those who employ investment advisers and broker/dealers want their own investment vehicles sold, but those investments, with their higher commissions, may not be in the best interest of the clients (Schwarcz 2005). Accuracy, full disclosure, and candor are important for mutual fund managers and investment clients alike. Sometimes, investment fund clients would prefer research that is less candid and more positive because they want the value of their investments preserved, but candor and duty to others in the markets (who are counting on transparency) demand a less-than-rosy outlook. Outlooks on optimism and candor vary depending on the client. Less optimism means share prices drop (Fisch 2006). Less optimism (more candor) is good news for those who avoid a purchase of the stock or who have not bought the stock yet but is often bad news for those who own the stock. Candor and optimism cannot always walk on the same side of the street.

There is one additional complication. The differences between the role of a broker and that of an investment adviser may seem clear to those within the profession, but the distinctions may escape their clients. Investment advisers are classified as fiduciaries who must act in the best interest of their clients, but brokers are not fiduciaries. That distinction survived and enjoyed regulatory allowances until the 1980s. However, over the past 30 years, the line between brokers and investment advisers has become increasingly blurred. There are now fee-based brokerage accounts, and more brokers refer to themselves as financial advisers.

As a result of this blurring of distinctions, ethical and legal standards for broker/dealers and investment advisers have been researched and debated, and yet the issues remain unresolved (Strier 2005). A US SEC study released in 2011 recommended that there be one uniform standard for broker/dealers and investment advisers.[2] SEC action on the recommendation is pending. However, even without an SEC rule, there are some standards from which all investment professionals could benefit regardless of their role. Through a review of market history, literature, and general principles from fiduciary

[2]The study was mandated by the Dodd–Frank Wall Street Reform and Consumer Protection Act of 2010. In addition, as will be discussed later, the US Department of Labor (DOL) is considering the imposition of new fiduciary standards in its area of jurisdiction—that of employer-sponsored retirement fund managers and advisers. The DOL also appears to be leaning toward adoption of the uniform fiduciary standard.

relationships, some simple concepts emerge that could help investment professionals navigate the conflicts of interest that are inevitable given the overlapping roles that they play in the financial markets. Following such voluntary paths could allow investment professionals a role in shaping the final regulations regarding the application of fiduciary duty standards to broker/dealers.

The Nature of Investment Markets

The current debates, regulatory proposals, and focus of reforms deal with the distinction (in a fiduciary sense) between investment advisers and broker/dealers. Both groups play large roles in the financial markets.

The number and types of investors have been expanding. At the end of 2012, there was $14.7 trillion in assets in the US financial markets held by 94 million US investors.[3] Approximately 52% of the US population invests in the stock market, and 44% of US households hold mutual fund investments.[4] These figures represent a low since the 2008 market collapse, and rising market confidence will result in increases in those numbers. These figures also indicate that investors are a diverse group, with many individual investors owning both individual stocks and mutual fund shares. Investors vary widely in their levels of knowledge and sophistication, but they all have one thing in common: They take market risk.

Who Are the Market's Advisers, and How Are They Regulated?

There is a long history associated with the role of advisers. From the time of the original federal securities law through ongoing statutory and regulatory reforms, the term "adviser" has evolved.

Original Investment Adviser and Broker/Dealer Regulation. The Securities Exchange Act of 1934 covers the secondary trading markets, including brokers and stock exchanges, but the expansion of investment vehicles to include mutual funds, closed-end funds, and investment trusts created a regulatory void that was filled by the passage of the Investment Company Act of 1940[5] (Slaughter 2014). This latter act addressed information verification and dissemination for investors in these new types of market offerings. By requiring that financials be audited and disseminated to investors, this act approached investor protection through disclosure and education.

[3]Lydia Saad, "U.S. Stock Ownership Stays at Record Low," *Gallup Economy* (8 May 2013): www.gallup.com/poll/162353/stock-ownership-stays-record-low.aspx.
[4]Ibid.
[5]15 USC §§ 80a-1–80a64 (1940).

The accompanying Investment Advisers Act of 1940 established a regulatory structure for monitoring advisers with the goal of protecting investors through asset protections and bans against self-dealing.[6]

These two acts provided a structure for registering both investment advisers and broker/dealers, as well as a code of ethics for professionals beyond statutory requirements. Investment advisers are subject to fiduciary standards and to the anti-fraud provisions of the Securities Act of 1933 and the Securities Exchange Act of 1934.[7] However, broker/dealers were specifically exempted from the fiduciary standards of the Investment Advisers Act if certain conditions were satisfied, including certain statutory requirements, self-regulation, and adoption of ethics codes. By 1939, investment professionals and investment firms had created the National Association of Securities Dealers (NASD), which was charged with the protection of investors through standards for and enforcement of open and honest conduct on the part of its members under the SEC's oversight. These types of self-regulatory organizations (SROs) assisted in the protection of investors in varying ways beyond their codes of ethics, including licensing, certification, and recovery funds. The NASD evolved into the Financial Industry Regulatory Authority (FINRA), which is a self-regulatory body. Broker/dealers who do business with the public are required to be registered with FINRA. Together, the SEC and FINRA oversee 5,100 broker/dealers. About 18% of the FINRA-registered broker/dealers are also registered as investment advisers under SEC rules.

The Regulatory Distinction between the Roles of Broker/Dealers and Investment Advisers and the Blurring of That Distinction. Under the framework initially established through federal regulation and the subsequently adopted codes of ethics, there is a clear differentiation of duties between broker/dealers and investment advisers.

An investment adviser is defined as

> any person who, for compensation, engages in the business of advising others, either directly or through publications or writings, as to the value of securities or as to the advisability of investing in, purchasing, or selling securities, or who, for compensation and as part of a regular business, issues or promulgates analyses or reports concerning securities.[8]

Under the original securities and investment adviser statutes, a broker is defined as a "person engaged in the business of effecting transactions in securities for

[6]15 USC §§ 80b-1–80b21 (1940).

[7]Securities Act of 1933, 15 USC § 77 et seq. (1933); Securities Exchange Act of 1934, 15 USC § 78c (1934).

[8]Investment Advisers Act of 1940, 15 USC § 80b-2, § 202(a)(11) (1940).

the account of others."[9] A dealer is defined as a "person engaged in the business of buying and selling securities for his own account."[10]

The distinction in the original statutes, then, was between those who buy and sell securities for others and those who provide advice. As markets and roles evolved, however, broker/dealers did indeed also provide advice. Nonetheless, they were excluded from the regulations that apply to investment advisers.

Under the federal statutory structure, as originally passed, the basic duty of the broker/dealer is suitability, a standard that is often referred to as one of fair dealing. No contractual relationship exists between broker/dealers and clients in which there is ongoing monitoring of the client's funds and investments. A broker/dealer may make a recommendation on a particular security, but once the transaction is complete, the broker/dealer receives no further compensation.

However, this statutory distinction has all but disappeared in practice. During the 1990s, broker/dealers began offering fee-based accounts to their customers. In fee-based brokerage accounts, broker/dealers "provide customers [with] a package of brokerage services—including execution, investment advice, custodial and record-keeping services—for a fee based on the amounts of assets on account with the broker-dealer" (quoted in Varnavides 2011[11]). These fee-based accounts and broker/dealer practices resulted in an SEC proposal to subject broker/dealers to investment adviser status. Because of pushback from broker/dealers, the SEC allowed the new fee structure and continued the exemption as long as the broker/dealers were offering advice that was only "incidental" to their brokerage services. However, a federal court ruled that this SEC-created expansion of the exemption for broker/dealers was an *ultra vires* act by the agency, a regulatory action that was beyond the scope and intent of the 1940 statutory framework and thus disallowed.[12]

The SEC discontinued its judicial battle over the rule and instead issued a new rule that included a three-part analysis that would be used to determine whether a broker/dealer was exempt from the Investment Advisers Act of 1940 liability standard for investment advisers:

- Advisory status would be determined on a case-by-case basis.
- Charging different commissions for different brokerage services would not automatically mean that a broker/dealer was receiving "special compensation" (indicating investment adviser status).

[9]Securities Exchange Act of 1934, 15 USC § 78c, § 3(a)(4)(A) (1934).
[10]Securities Exchange Act of 1934, 15 USC § 78c, § 3(a)(5)(A) (1934).
[11]Quoted text is from Clint A. Corrie, "Investment Advisers and Brokers: When Is a Broker Subject to Fiduciary Duties?," in Practicing Law Institute Course Handbook Series, Securities Arbitration Institute (August 2009).
[12]Financial Planning Association v. SEC, 482 F.3d 481 (D.C. Cir. 2007).

- A broker/dealer who exercised investment discretion beyond limited or temporary discretion would be considered an investment adviser and would be subject to the Investment Advisers Act.[13]

As these interpretive guidelines have been applied judicially, an overall accepted standard has evolved. If the advice the broker/dealer gives is "solely incidental to the conduct of his business as a broker or dealer" and the broker/dealer receives no "special compensation" for the advice given, then he or she is not an investment adviser in a legal sense.[14] The courts have concluded that, although a broker/dealer will always give a certain amount of advice to clients, the congressional focus in the 1940 legislation was not on broker/dealers and the expansion of fiduciary duties to this group but on those whose principal business was as investment advisers. The courts' interpretation of the exemption is that if there is a commission payment arrangement, the exemption applies, regardless of the type of advice or even the pressure that the broker/dealer might be feeling to sell certain stocks.[15]

There is one additional wrinkle in the case law that signals growing intolerance of broker/dealer behavior that harms a client; this point is grounded in the basic ethical principle of conflicts of interest. In *Thomas v. Metropolitan Life Insurance Company*, the court found that a broker/dealer who was not managing an account for a client, not taking a fee for managing the account (beyond commissions), and not involved in any special relationship with the client did not owe a fiduciary duty to that client.[16] However, in this case, the broker/dealer had sold the client certain investment vehicles that entitled him to a higher commission than if he had sold the client similar vehicles sponsored by a firm other than his own. The court's opinion is an important one because although the decision supported the view that there was no fiduciary duty, the dictum in the case indicates that the interpretation and application of the 1940 regulatory structure might not protect a broker/dealer who did not disclose a compensation differential to the client. The case indicates a judicial discomfort with a policy under which broker/dealers are entitled to the exemption except in situations involving so basic an ethical breach as a conflict of interest. The court was struck by the fact that the broker/dealer in this case was performing the same functions as an investment adviser but was exempt from the

[13]SEC, "Certain Broker-Dealers Deemed Not to Be Investment Advisers," 17 CFR 275, Release No. 34-51523, 70 Fed. Reg. 240424-01 (19 April 2005).
[14]15 USC § 80b-2(a)(11)(C) (1940).
[15]Thomas v. Metropolitan Life Insurance Company, 631 F.3d 1153, 1164 (10th Cir. 2011). The SEC supported the judicial position at 17 CFR § 275. (However, that support was issued before the release of the Dodd–Frank study.)
[16]Thomas v. Metropolitan Life Insurance Company, 2009 WL 2778663, Fed. Sec. L. Rep. P 95,344 (W.D. Okla. 2009); 631 F.3d 1153, 1164 (10th Cir. 2011).

investment adviser's fiduciary standards. The delineation appeared arbitrary to the court, and its opinion made clear that something needed to be done about that arbitrary distinction.

The distinction between investment advisers and broker/dealers has become increasingly blurred. To add to the confusion between fiduciary and nonfiduciary conduct, the structure of investment firms has shifted. In the 1940s, broker/dealers and investment advisers were separate and did not overlap. Today, however, an investment adviser may or may not be affiliated with a broker. There is no clear differentiation of duties in the definitions, and physically, brokers, dealers, and advisers often operate under the same investment firm roof. Data from the SEC study indicate that 88% of investment advisers are also registered as broker/dealers.[17] The SEC has also found that 34% of retail-level investors view the primary function of broker/dealers as "giving advice."[18]

Certain exceptions have sprung from judicial decisions, and there are also SRO rules that expand on the notions of suitability and fair dealing (discussed later).[19]

An additional complication of the broker/dealer versus investment adviser issue has been created by the use of yet another layer of professionals who work with clients. Broker/dealers use stockbrokers to interact with clients. Those stockbrokers are agents of the broker/dealers and thus by common law agency standards owe a duty of loyalty to their principal, the broker/dealer. That duty to the principal trumps any duties owed to the clients placing orders. This situation adds to investors' confusion about the roles and responsibilities of the various parties with whom they interact.

The Scope of the Investment Adviser's Fiduciary Duty. In contrast to the evolving and murky duties of broker/dealers, the scope of liability of investment advisers is fairly clear under the original federal statutes and has remained so since their passage. An investment adviser is classified as a fiduciary with a role defined both by codes of ethics for the profession and by the SEC. An adviser does not just recommend stocks; an adviser is obligated to monitor a client's account and keep the client informed about changes in risk and the status of the securities in the client's account. Several basic standards apply to this fiduciary role (Wrona 2012).

---

[17]SEC, "Study on Investment Advisers and Broker-Dealers as Required by Section 913 of the Dodd–Frank Wall Street Reform and Consumer Protection Act" (January 2011); hereafter referred to as "SEC study."

[18]SEC study, p. 100.

[19]For example, following the investor losses owing to derivative investments in the 1990s, some courts imposed duties of disclosure on broker/dealers by holding them liable for their failure to explain the complexities and risks of such investments (Buerstetta 1996).

Duty of care. The investment adviser is required to provide only "suitable" investment advice—that is, advice suitable to the specific client being advised. The suitability standard has not been articulated well by the SEC and is better defined by FINRA. The basic obligation is for the adviser to be sure that any recommendation made to a client is appropriate for that client's individual situation and objectives.

Another aspect of the duty of care requires the adviser to select the best broker/dealer to execute a client's transactions under the circumstances. Under this standard, an adviser can use an affiliated broker/dealer as long as the conflict is disclosed. Included under this duty is the prohibition on trading ahead of customer orders.

Duty of loyalty. Investment advisers are to serve the best interest of the client. Translated, this duty means that an investment adviser must not profit on his or her (or the firm's) investments at the expense of the client. The fiduciary duty of investment advisers includes the duty of loyalty. Under the duty of loyalty, the investment adviser must manage conflicts of interest with clients by withdrawal, elimination of the conflict, or full disclosure of the conflict. Full disclosure means revelation to the client of all material facts, such as whether the adviser or the adviser's firm stands to profit from the client's investing in certain products.

There is an extensive body of case law dealing with investment advisers' fiduciary duty. However, the US Supreme Court established the breadth of the fiduciary standard in an early case that dealt with the history and intent of the 1940 legislation and concluded that the "fundamental purpose" of the Investment Advisers Act was "to achieve a high standard of business ethics in the securities industry."[20]

The Investment Advisers Act also includes some prohibitions on conduct by advisers. For example, an adviser, acting as principal for its own account, cannot make a sale or purchase for a client without first disclosing, in writing, the adviser's conflicting interests and obtaining the written consent of the client.

Securities Exchange Act of 1934: Liability for Advisers and Broker/Dealers. Advisers and broker/dealers are also subject to generic market regulations. Both advisers and broker/dealers can be held liable for investor losses, not on the basis of a breach of fiduciary duty but on the condition that the investor can establish the following conduct and results under Rule 10b of the Securities Exchange Act of 1934:[21]

- The broker/dealer or investment adviser has made misrepresentations or omissions of material facts about the purchase or sale of securities for the client.

[20]SEC v. Capital Gains Research Bureau, 375 US 180, 186 (1963).
[21]15 USC § 78u-4 (1934).

- The broker/dealer or investment adviser made the misrepresentations knowing that they were false.
- The client reasonably relied on those misrepresentations.
- The client experienced a loss as a result of reliance on the broker/dealer or investment adviser.

Liability under securities law is dependent on representations or affirmative action by a broker/dealer or adviser and not on the failure to fulfill an assigned fiduciary duty. This type of liability applies to anyone who engages in misrepresentation or omission of information in the sale or purchase of securities. Imposed on both broker/dealers and investment advisers, this is a generic duty that applies to all who trade in securities—the duty to not defraud clients or investors.

Subsequent Investment Adviser and Broker/Dealer Regulation. The original 1940 statutes have been supplemented. For example, the Employment Retirement Income Security Act (ERISA)[22] provides specific rules and duties for certain fund managers, is administered by the Department of Labor, and thus differs from the SEC-administered securities and investment company statutes. Under ERISA, investment managers who serve as pension plan fiduciaries for employer-sponsored retirement plans have four duties: (1) the duty of loyalty to plan participants; (2) the duty to make prudent investments; (3) the duty of diversification to minimize losses; and (4) a duty to adhere to the provisions, directions, and limitations in the employer plan documents.

SRO Duties. Beyond the statutory responsibilities and regulations, broker/dealers are subject to FINRA rules (some of which were originally NASD rules) that explain the levels of care and duties owed to clients. In lieu of the statutory fiduciary standard to which investment advisers are held, the FINRA rules flesh out the following duties of broker/dealers under the fair-dealing standard imposed by statute:

- The suitability standard. There must be a reasonable basis for recommendations to clients—that is, the broker/dealer must show reasonable diligence in evaluating investments and applying suitability standards (NASD Rule 2310; NASD Rule 2111, which requires reasonable-basis suitability, quantitative suitability, and suitability as applied to the individual client).
- Fair and balanced communications with the public (NASD Rule 2210[d]).
- Timely confirmation of transactions (NASD Rule 2340).

[22] 29 USC §§ 1001–1461 (1974).

- Disclosure of conflicts of interest (NASD Rule 2720; NASD Rule 3040).
- Fair compensation (NASD Rule 2440; FINRA Rule 5110[c]).
- Resolution of disputes with clients through arbitration.

SRO duties are continually changed and expanded. For example, FINRA has expanded Suitability Rule 2111, which now requires broker/dealers to obtain full information about their clients, including the client's investment goals and objectives, risk tolerance, net worth, income, and tax bracket. The background information must be certified by the client, and the broker/dealer has a duty to make recommendations that are appropriate for the parameters certified by the client. Additional FINRA rules place disclosure requirements on broker/dealers, and although the details are beyond the scope of this discussion, it is important to note that FINRA continues to expand the disclosure requirements of broker/dealers.[23]

Other SROs have also imposed fiduciary standards. For example, the Certified Financial Planner Board of Standards requires those who attain the group's certification to use a fiduciary standard of care in dealing with clients.

State Laws. There are four states that impose fiduciary duties on broker/dealers. The states are permitted to impose a standard that is higher than federal standards; the states cannot, however, impose a lesser standard. A fiduciary duty established at the federal level cannot be eliminated at the state level.

Negligence and Common Law Duties: Judicial Interpretations. Over the years, a rich body of case law has developed because clients of broker/dealers have attempted to use common law standards of negligence (i.e., breach of duty) to impose liability (Hurt 2014). Whether these common law theories have resulted in broker/dealer liability has depended on the nature of the client's relationship.

One of the factors that determine judicial willingness to impose broker/dealer liability is the type of account. For example, if the client holds a nondiscretionary account with a broker/dealer, there is no duty to monitor on the part of the broker/dealer and no duty to inform the client generally about market risks or changing market patterns.[24] The duties are limited to best execution of trades, and the advice given on a particular transaction does not

[23]For example, as a result of the 2008 market collapse, in 2009, FINRA began requiring that broker/dealers who sell REITs disclose the market value of those REITs on client statements. The post-2008 market values have been significantly lower than the original investment values because of the real estate market collapse.

[24]Welch v. TD Ameritrade Holding Corporation, No. 07 Civ. 6904 (RJS), 2009 WL 2356131 (S.D.N.Y. 2009).

constitute an assumption of responsibility for the continued monitoring of the securities involved in that transaction or any additional monitoring of the client's account.

Courts have been willing to carve out some exceptions to the exemption from fiduciary duty liability for broker/dealers in nondiscretionary account situations. Those exceptions, called "transformative special circumstances," involve situations in which the client is impaired or the broker/dealer has undertaken something more than an arm's-length relationship with the client.[25]

Courts have imposed fiduciary duties on broker/dealers who are handling discretionary accounts for clients. In some cases, however, the courts rely on state law provisions that impose such liability on broker/dealers.[26]

Dodd–Frank Changes. The most recent changes to the original statutory framework spring from the so-called Dodd–Frank legislation. Passed following the 2008 market collapse, Dodd–Frank (the Wall Street Reform and Consumer Protection Act of 2010) amended certain provisions of the 1940 Advisers Act with a directive to the SEC to study the issues involved in and obtain public opinions about broker/dealers' being subject to a fiduciary duty when advising retail and institutional investors.[27] This possible expansion of fiduciary duty to broker/dealers (even at the institutional level) is the result of congressional and public reaction to testimony at the congressional hearings on Dodd–Frank.

One of the debates that ensued during the congressional hearings on Dodd–Frank, following the 2008 financial market collapse, was over whether an investment firm—namely, Goldman Sachs—owed a fiduciary duty to clients who were purchasing investment vehicles through Goldman when Goldman held short positions in those same mortgage-backed securities. Goldman held those short positions because it had advance knowledge that the investments were likely to fall in value because of its involvement in the selection of the firm that structured the pool of mortgages underlying the investment vehicles Goldman was then selling to clients. Goldman had arranged for an outside consultant to pick the mortgages for the investment pool and was aware of their poor quality. The outside consultant was not aware of Goldman's plan to position itself (by selling short) to profit from a deal it was structuring and, indeed, was confused by the selection of lower-quality mortgages for the pool.[28]

[25]Welch v. TD Ameritrade Holding Corporation, 306 F.3d 1293 (2nd Cir. 2002).

[26]Marchese v. Nelson, 809 F. Supp. 880 (D. Utah 1993); Lautenberg Foundation v. Madoff, Civil Action No. 09-816 (SRC), 2009 WL 2928913 (D.N.J. 2009), at 7.

[27]The SEC study has been completed and recommends extension of the fiduciary responsibility. The study's recommendations are discussed in detail later in this article.

[28]Gretchen Morgenson and Louise Story, "Banks Bundled Debt, Bet Against It and Won," *New York Times* (24 December 2009):A1, B4.

During the hearings on Dodd–Frank and the issue of fiduciary duty as applied to broker/dealers, witnesses from Goldman Sachs made clear that the firm was not acting as an investment adviser in selling the mortgage-backed securities. Rather, Goldman took the position that it was simply selling securities and taking orders for the purchase of those securities. Under the laws and regulations at that time, including the definitive distinction between the levels and types of duty of broker/dealers and those of investment advisers, Goldman was not in a fiduciary relationship with those purchasing the Goldman-underwritten investment vehicles. As a result, there was no legal requirement that Goldman act in the best interest of its clients.

However, in a frank and stunning memo written to its clients in January 2010, Goldman Sachs admitted that it often made recommendations to clients for investments in which Goldman had already positioned itself short. The memo read, in part, "We may trade, and have existing positions, based on trading ideas before we have discussed those ideas with you."[29] The disclosure of Goldman's contra-client positions had appeared in the fine print in the firm's marketing materials, but the memo represented the first time that Goldman had discussed these positions affirmatively with its clients. Again, under the law at the time, Goldman had complied with its duties as a broker/dealer.

Perhaps more than any other evidence at the hearing, the testimony of Lloyd Blankfein, chairman and CEO of Goldman Sachs, was the catalyst for the expansion of the fiduciary duty standard to broker/dealers. Mr. Blankfein was questioned about Goldman's failure to disclose the conflict of interest related to its retention of a firm to select the mortgages for a pool of collateralized debt obligations (CDOs)—selections that were, as one commentator phrased it, "dogs" and that Goldman employees referred to as "s——y" or "crappy."[30] Mr. Blankfein testified that Goldman Sachs had no fiduciary duty to disclose the conflict or Goldman's position in the investment vehicles. Then-Senator Carl Levin had the following exchange with Mr. Blankfein:

> Senator Levin: In a deal where you are selling securities and you are intending to keep the short side of that deal, which is what happened here in a lot of these deals, do you think you have an obligation to tell the person that you're selling that security to in that deal that you are keeping the short position in that deal? . . .
>
> Mr. Blankfein: I don't think we would disclose that. . . . If a client came to us and asked us to buy something from him and we intended to hold the

[29]Andrew Ross Sorkin, "At Goldman, E-Mail Message Lays Bare Conflicts in Trading," *New York Times* (13 January 2010):B1.

[30]Michael M. Phillips, "Senators Seek, Fail to Get an 'I'm Sorry,'" *Wall Street Journal* (28 April 2010):A3, A5.

long position, I don't think we have an obligation of telling him that our intention is to hold it. . . . We are buying from sellers and selling to buyers. . . . That is not a conflict. . . . They wouldn't care what our views are.[31]

Another Goldman executive, Daniel Sparks, was asked, "Do you have a duty to act in the best interests of your clients?" Mr. Sparks replied, "I believe we have a duty to serve our clients well."[32]

Earlier in the hearing, in his prepared remarks, Mr. Blankfein said, "What we and other banks, rating agencies and regulators failed to do was sound the alarm that there was too much lending and too much leverage in the system—that credit had become too cheap."[33]

The hearing proved to be a watershed moment in the move to impose a fiduciary standard on broker/dealers. Following the hearing and the Goldman Sachs testimony, the only issue that appeared to be unresolved was the parameters of broker/dealers' fiduciary duty. There was disagreement in both the House and the Senate over the scope of the duty and its application.

Following the hearing, several senators proposed legislative changes that would impose a fiduciary duty on broker/dealers in situations where there is a disparity of expertise, in derivatives transactions, and in broker/dealers' relationships with pension plans, employee benefit plans, and state and local governments. One proposed bill would have criminalized the failure to make certain disclosures. The disagreements over application and scope found Congress punting. The legislation in Dodd–Frank relating to the fiduciary duty of broker/dealers left the issue unresolved and transferred the final decisions and drafting of the fiduciary standards to the SEC via a study mandate. Under Dodd–Frank, the SEC was to examine the following issues:

- The effectiveness of existing legal and regulatory standards of care (imposed by the SEC, private regulators, and other federal or state authorities) for providing personalized investment advice and recommendations about securities to retail customers
- Whether there are legal or regulatory gaps, shortcomings, or overlaps in those legal and regulatory standards that should be addressed by rule or statute

[31]Sara Hansard, "Blankfein and Levin Spar over Goldman Sachs's Market Maker Role," *DailyFinance* (27 April 2010): www.dailyfinance.com/2010/04/27/blankfein-and-levin-spar-over-goldman-sachss-market-maker-role (retrieved 16 May 2014).

[32]Richard Adams, "Goldman Sachs Senate Hearing: As It Happened," *Guardian* (27 April 2010): www.theguardian.com/business/richard-adams-blog/2010/apr/27/goldman-sachs-senate-hearing-live-blog.

[33]*Hearing on Wall Street and the Financial Crisis: The Role of Investment Banks, before the Permanent Subcomm. on Investigations, Comm. on Homeland Security and Governmental Affairs,* US Senate, statement of Lloyd C. Blankfein, chairman of the board and chief executive officer, Goldman Sachs Group, Inc. (27 April 2010).

That study has been completed and concludes with a recommendation for the imposition of a fiduciary duty on broker/dealers. The study's conclusion is based on the following findings by the SEC staff:

- Investors are confused about the roles played by investment advisers and broker/dealers.
- Many investors are also confused about the standards of care that apply to investment advisers and broker/dealers.
- It is burdensome for investors to have to "parse" legal language to determine what kinds of advice they are entitled to from investment advisers and broker/dealers.
- Uniformity of duties on the part of investment advisers and broker/dealers is necessary to prevent investor confusion.
- The uniform fiduciary standard from the Investor Advisers Act should be applied to broker/dealers.

The Shifts in Registration and Regulatory Supervision. An additional Dodd–Frank change that modified the 1940 legislation substantially was the reallocation of the primary responsibility for oversight of investment advisers. The SEC, under Dodd–Frank, has delegated to the states the responsibility for regulating advisers that have between $25 million and $100 million of assets under management. However, Dodd–Frank transferred supervision of advisers whose assets under management are $100 million and larger to the federal government. Dodd–Frank also repealed the "private adviser exemption."

As of October 2012, there were 11,002 investment advisers registered with the SEC, with 37% advising hedge funds and other private funds. That total represented an increase of 1,504 registered advisers since the SEC passed the regulatory changes regarding investment adviser registration mandated under Dodd–Frank.[34] In addition, as required under the expanded Dodd–Frank regulations, 2,300 midsize advisers (firms with more than $100 million in assets) made the transition from state registration to federal (SEC) registration. These expansions of registration requirements mean that more advisers now fall under the SEC's fiduciary standards and requirements. Approximately 5% of SEC-registered investment advisers are also registered as broker/dealers, and 22% have a related person who is a broker/dealer. Additionally, approximately 88% of investment adviser representatives are also registered representatives of broker/dealers. Most investment advisers

[34]The rules that implemented the expanded registration requirements of Dodd–Frank became effective in September 2011 and can be found at 17 CFR Parts 275 and 279.

charge their clients fees based on a percentage of assets under management, while others may charge hourly or fixed rates.

This market structure is emphasized here because at least one SEC commissioner has pointed to the antiquated regulations for investment advisers and broker/dealers, referring to them "as a 'badly worn patchwork quilt' in desperate need of reform" (Varnavides 2011, p. 204). The laws and regulations are applied as if the structure of separate entities for advisers and broker/dealers still exists. With these professionals no longer "balkanized" into separate entities and roles, the statutory and regulatory provisions are obsolete (Varnavides 2011). The same commissioner has also noted that investment advisers and broker/dealers "often provide practically indistinguishable services to retail investors and direct them to the same [financial] products."[35]

Where to Now? Fiduciary Duty, or Not?

In addition to determining the effectiveness and adequacy of existing legal and regulatory standards for investment advice and recommendations, Dodd–Frank required the SEC to examine the following issues in financial markets as it considered the possible move to impose the fiduciary standard on broker/dealers:

- Whether retail customers understand or are confused by the differences in the standards of care that apply to broker/dealers and investment advisers
- The available resources for regulating, examining, and enforcing standards of care
- The potential impact on retail customers if regulatory requirements change, including customers' access to the range of products and services offered by broker/dealers
- The potential impact of eliminating the broker/dealer exclusion from the definition of "investment adviser" under the Investment Advisers Act of 1940
- The potential additional costs to retail customers, broker/dealers, and investment advisers that would result from changes in regulatory requirements

The first issue has been discussed and dismissed as a nonissue: The SEC study concluded that investors are indeed confused by the differences in standards. The second issue was also resolved by the study, which concluded that the SEC has the necessary resources to enforce the ramping up of the fiduciary standard to the broker/dealer level. However, the remaining three

[35]Elisse B. Walter, "Regulating Broker-Dealers and Investment Advisers: Demarcation or Harmonization?," Presentation given at the Mutual Fund Directors Forum Ninth Annual Policy Conference (5 May 2009): www.sec.gov/news/speech/2009/spch050509ebw.htm.

issues have not been resolved. Indeed, there are significant studies and views regarding the impact on retail customers of changing to a fiduciary standard, the effect on costs for all market stakeholders, and the impact on the market, remedies, and customer protections. The following sections provide a summary of the various studies, concerns, and findings regarding the proposal to change to a fiduciary standard for brokers and dealers.

The Economic Impact of Changing to a Fiduciary Standard. Economics can be described as the science of understanding the consequences of imposing additional costs on one group. As the focus on investor protections takes hold, the perceived benefits of proposed reforms often overshadow the unintended, but very real, costs and consequences of expanded regulation. Requiring broker/dealers to be subject to a fiduciary standard would impose additional costs on this group as well as on their firms. One consequence of the additional duties, risks, and liabilities would be higher costs for retail investors. Broker/dealers could raise their commissions in order to cover the cost of the additional risks. Walsh and Johns (2013) summarized this concern:

> A commission based compensation scheme cannot support adherence to a fiduciary duty imposed on a broker-dealer. Thus, broker-dealers would most likely move to a percentage fee charged against assets under management model to support the enhanced requirements of the fiduciary duty. In order to make money, broker-dealers will require minimum assets for them to manage, just like investment advisers require. The small investor will not have the assets needed to get professional recommendations and advice until they are able to grow their own accounts perhaps through the use of online brokerage firms. Only individuals with sizable assets will be able to obtain the assistance of a broker or investment adviser. (p. 447)

Add to this decline in services the generic impact of universal protections for buyers/investors. When investors have a healthy dose of skepticism, they tend to do their own research and make better decisions (Ben-Shahar and Schneider 2011). When confronted with a salesperson, a buyer or investor instinctively questions "puffery," shops around with other vendors, and seeks out additional advice before making a purchase.[36] Reliance on fiduciary standards may lessen the instinctive self-protective work that does allow buyers/investors to screen out bad products (Prentice 2011).

Another potential cost is that compliance with disclosure requirements would reduce the speed with which broker/dealers could complete

[36]Morgan Clemons, "Harmonization vs. Demarcation: The Problems with a Broker Fiduciary Duty and the Benefits of the Merrill Rule," working paper (October 2010): http://papers.ssrn.com/sol3/papers.cfm?abstract_id=1699274.

transactions.[37] Being certain that all disclosures were made and all compliance processes complete prior to a transaction would slow down the speed with which clients could trade (Lin 2014).

Easterbrook and Fischel (1993) argue that one impact of the imposition of fiduciary duty would be the loss of the ability to negotiate rights and obligations individually under contract law. Their theory is that the imposition of absolute duties deprives individuals of the ability to contract according to their needs. They advance the notion that sometimes self-interest permits the structuring of new market instruments with greater risk, where this risk is one that some investors may wish to take and can manage through customized contracting.

However, there is also the possibility that broker/dealers and their firms would find ways to minimize those additional costs or avoid application of the regulation (Easterbrook and Fischel 1993). One way to avoid the imposition of liability for advice is to refrain from giving advice. If broker/dealers ceased giving advice, especially to retail investors, this particular client group would be left without access to the information they once had. There are other ways that firms could attempt to avoid application of the fiduciary standard. For example, some firms might spin off a separate brokerage arm, thus separating the broker/dealers from the rest of the firm and eliminating the confusion on the part of investors that was an impetus for the change (Romano 1993). This new firm structure would carry a banner of "No advice here. Only orders." Again, retail investors would be cut out of an information and advice loop. The rise of low-cost discount and online brokers is a fulfillment of this forecast.

Another behavioral reaction could be broker/dealers seeking waivers from clients. In exchange for advice, the clients would agree to a different standard of duty, and the disclosure would include all of the activities broker/dealers could engage in before modification of the fiduciary standard (i.e., the activities they engage in today; Lin 2014). The waiver process would also introduce additional costs because of the time, paperwork, and recordkeeping requirements.

Root Cause: Why Is Regulation Looming, and Can the Course Be Changed?

Despite the costs of imposing fiduciary duty standards on broker/dealers and the study results indicating that this action may not accomplish legislators' and regulators' goals of improving retail investors' advice from broker/dealers, knowledge, and decision making, it seems that we are on an inexorable march in that direction.

[37]Arthur B. Laby, "Reforming the Regulation of Broker-Dealers and Investment Advisers," *Business Lawyer*, vol. 65, no. 2 (February 2010):395–440.

The investment industry is experiencing the final phase of the regulatory cycle, a cycle that moves toward regulation despite issues of cost and in defiance of information and research that demonstrate that the regulation will not be effective. The push to adopt a fiduciary standard for broker/dealers is the result of inaction and abuses within the financial industry that culminated with the Goldman Sachs testimony already highlighted in the discussion of the Dodd–Frank hearings.

Every business statute or regulation that presently exists began as an ethical dilemma. The political science model developed by James Frierson posits a sequence of events called the "regulatory cycle." Depicted in **Figure 1**, the cycle represents the phases through which an issue progresses from the time of its appearance as an ethical dilemma to its eventual fate as a subject of legislation, regulation, or adjudication.

When ethical issues arise and are not yet subject to statutory resolution, businesses and industries enjoy wide latitude regarding those issues. Some members of the profession or industry will seize the unregulated moment a bit too aggressively. Goldman's testimony about its view of the duty it owed to clients (as a broker/dealer) is a classic illustration of the seizure of an unregulated area to one's advantage. But the field of finance demands trust and a standard higher than simply "This is what the law allows."

The aggressive seizure of a loophole by some market participants means that other, more ethical participants will be at a disadvantage. The disadvantaged parties are those who participate in markets under the assumption that their trust in the markets is justified and that they, as market participants,

Figure 1. Regulatory Cycle: Options and Cost

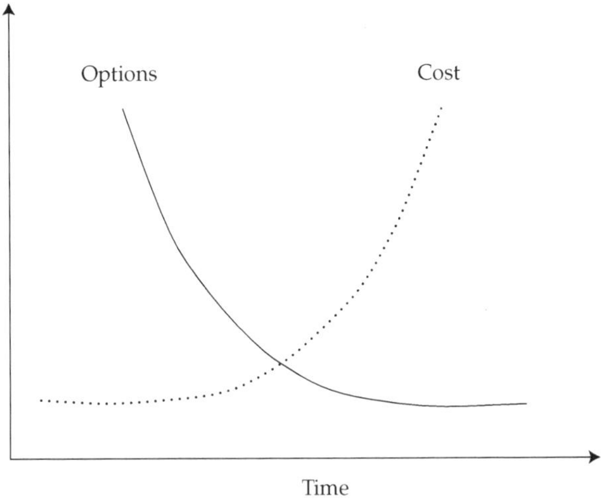

are not trying to take advantage of asymmetrical information. Honest people often assume that a common ethical standard exists in their marketplace. The existence of the regulatory cycle theory, based on examples from all industries, indicates that honest market participants are, too often, wrong in their assumptions about the ethical standards of others (Jennings 1992).

This misunderstanding about the ethical rules of the industry in the initial stage of the cycle inevitably results in the harms and losses that come from asymmetrical information distribution. "How was I to know that you held positions in these securities different from mine?" "How could I have known that you were putting together the pools of mortgages?" When the harm and investment losses come, those who trusted seize the moral high ground and take their case to the public. The public is sympathetic because its assumptions about markets are often identical to those of the parties who experienced the losses. Armed not with loopholes in the Investment Advisers Act but with the simple standards of ethics and fiduciary duty, the complainants are able to prosecute their cases against the investment managers and achieve increased regulation. They appeal to the emotions that naturally arise when one is betrayed by a trusted party. The resulting sympathy for the victim and outrage at the perpetrator drive the regulatory cycle. Data are largely irrelevant as the cycle progresses toward the regulation phase.

Figure 1 illustrates the behavior of options for self-regulation and costs over time. The longer companies and industries wait to take self-corrective action, the less likely their self-correction will be allowed and the more likely regulators will impose regulation—often with unintended consequences, including additional costs. The firm's costs increase with the length of time it takes to address the evolving issues.

The Stages and Activities of the Regulatory Cycle

In the latency stage of the cycle, market and industry participants enjoy plenty of options for handling a loophole or gray area. During this phase of the cycle, only those in the industry—and perhaps academics and researchers—are aware of the evolving issue. For example, the issue of fiduciary duty (as suggested in the Bibliography) was for many years a topic of academic research and writing and was certainly understood within financial markets and firms. Analysts, researchers, and even some investment firms expressed concerns about disclosures, sales techniques, and ways of structuring or positioning in deals that could harm retail investors and other customers. But the issue remained of interest only to those in the financial field. The application of fiduciary duties to broker/dealers failed to gain traction in general-interest newspapers or weekly news magazines.

Every issue continues through the regulatory cycle following this initial latency phase. The awareness stage begins when the popular press reports on an issue and begins to raise questions and discuss how the issue affects the public. Once the public has knowledge of a potential problem, it responds by demanding assurance either that there is no problem or that the problem can be solved.

If that assurance or resolution is not forthcoming, the public takes the issue to the activism stage by calling for reform. In the activism stage, members of the public, special-interest groups, and victims who were harmed by inaction in the latency and awareness stages ask for either voluntary or regulatory reform. At this point, these groups tend to favor regulatory reform because they see that voluntary reform has not been undertaken to resolve the issue, despite general awareness and widespread publicity. In short, the public loses faith in a company's or industry's willingness to change its behavior, practices, or products.

If voluntary reform is not forthcoming, the issue moves into the litigation, legislative, or regulatory (administrative agency) stage. Options decrease because resolution is no longer simply a matter of answering to the public or those who were harmed. Regulators and legislators have their own ideas about how to fix the problem, and past inaction leaves the industry or company with a lesser voice in this stage of the cycle. Outrage is fueled by extreme conduct in unregulated areas. If the conduct is not addressed by the industry or profession, regulation comes, and it has come with each market blowup since the Enron issues of 2001.

In the case of broker/dealer responsibilities to clients and calls for the imposition of fiduciary duties, the 2008 market collapse moved the issue very quickly from the latency stage through the public awareness stage to activism, leaving it (for several years now) in the regulatory phase. The public, investors, and political figures have demanded reform of the duty broker/dealers owe to their clients. Suddenly, the issue of fiduciary duty, one that had occupied the halls of academia since the 1940s, was being covered in *USA Today*.[38] The public suddenly had an interest in the nuances of defining investment advisers versus broker/dealers and how loopholes worked to the advantage of investment firms in terms of required disclosures.

Congressional hearings began, Dodd–Frank was passed, and the SEC is now poised to change the broker/dealer standard of responsibility to a fiduciary duty. Goldman Sachs's defiant position in the Dodd–Frank hearings regarding its duty to its clients may have been legally correct at that time, but it sparked a revolt. Goldman did not realize that at this stage of the regulatory cycle, defiance does not play well. However, an industry can still have input into regulatory changes during this final stage.

[38]David J. Lynch, "Goldman Hearings Strike a Defiant Note," *USA Today* (28 April 2010):1B.

Is It Too Late? Strategies for the Final Stage of the Cycle

The goal of self-control during the progressions of the regulatory cycle is to build a "vibrant and dynamic" financial system that "won't blow up and drag the whole world down every few years" (Rogers 2014, p. 6). At present, the industry appears to be somewhat defiant about the SEC's adoption of the recommendation to expand the fiduciary standard to broker/dealers, in the sense that there still seems to be a belief that this process can be halted. The hard truth is that industry concerns about market impact and costs to investors are accurate. Another hard truth is that additional disclosure and liability standards do not always produce better outcomes for investors (Coffee 2004). Indeed, overreliance by investors on statutory disclosures and protections diverts them from the difficult and responsible effort of studying investment opportunities and making suitable investment choices. Again, data and hard truths do not move the regulatory cycle. Emotions carry the day, and the cycle moves forward. The conduct and events that led to the 2008 market crash—even if not all market professionals engaged in that conduct or those events—have been used to paint a picture that allows regulatory expansion and increased liability.

However, some strategies can be used in the final phase of the regulatory cycle that would give the industry a chance to influence what form the new regulation will take. Broker/dealers and investment advisers should take part in shaping that regulation to minimize the economic consequences and harm to investors that have already been outlined.

The key to the efficacy of these strategies, in terms of shaping the eventual content of the regulation on fiduciary duty, is for the industry to acknowledge that there are issues that require behavior modification and then offer solutions to address those issues, thus limiting overly broad regulatory strokes that may not focus on these critical issues. Acknowledging that bad behaviors have occurred in the industry is a means of establishing credibility and earning a seat at the rule-making table.

Focus on the Type of Investor to Be Protected. Bai (2014) suggests that subjecting broker/dealers to a fiduciary standard will have only a limited effect on institutional investors:

> Fiduciary duties comparable to that borne by investment advisers entails a duty to disclose material facts (including conflicts of interest), a duty not to subordinate the interests of clients to the interests of the broker-dealers, and a duty to use reasonable diligence to avoid making unsuitable recommendations. Such duties are already covered in the existing securities statutes and FINRA's suitability rules, and broker-dealers are held liable for violating them, either intentionally or negligently, just as investment advisers are. The only scenario in which broker-dealers probably face a reduced duty of care to an institutional

> client is when FINRA's suitability exemption applies, in which case broker-dealers are relieved from performing a suitability analysis for the client. (p. 100)

Thus, a possible contribution to the rule making would be to emphasize the scope of SRO standards and the coverage for investors there. As this discussion about existing protections progresses, the rule making could be refocused to answer these questions: Which investors are we trying to protect? Where does that protection need to be provided? How can we best narrow the scope to afford that protection without increasing costs or eliminating services for those investors? (Lydenberg 2014).

This discussion could include, for example, allowing institutional investors to waive proposed broker/dealer fiduciary duties by an agreement. There is precedent for such limitations because the SEC has permitted investment advisers to modify an adviser's liabilities through a hedge clause.[39] As this discussion proceeds, the opportunity may arise to expand the availability of waivers to retail investors who meet certain standards. There is precedent under the Securities Act of 1933 for allowing disclosure exemptions and even forgoing the registration process for investors who meet certain standards of income and asset levels.

Focus on Defining the Duties of Broker/Dealers. Another strategy at this stage of the cycle would be to concentrate on the conduct that has created the emotional drivers for the imposition of fiduciary duties on broker/dealers. As an alternative to a generic fiduciary standard that will continue to need interpretation and judicial application, this stage of the cycle is amenable to proposals that address the specific conduct that spawned the cycle's progression into outrage.

In many of the cases of broker/dealer litigation discussed in this review, as well as in the Dodd–Frank hearings themselves, the conduct of the broker/dealers was shocking from an ethical perspective (Angel and McCabe 2013). Shock moves the cycle. Halting the behaviors that caused the shock pulls the cycle back to a more reflective mode and reduces its speed. The industry can then focus on specific conduct; for example, the requirement to disclose that you can make a higher commission by selling your own company's products to investors is a basic ethical tenet that should be followed regardless of statutory requirements. For the sake of building client trust, this type of disclosure is and always has been necessary. Likewise, letting your client know that the investment vehicle you are recommending is one in which you carry a short position is not an ethical gray area. That information needs to be disclosed, regardless of any statutory duty.

Perhaps what is needed is not an imposed general fiduciary standard but, rather, a basic set of rules that apply across the investment markets,

[39]Heitman Capital Management, LLC, SEC No-Action Letter, LEXIS 159, at 25–28, 30–31 (12 February 2007).

regardless of the role played by a given individual or institution in those markets. Additional regulation has resulted in an overreliance on rules and a departure from basic ethical standards.

One reform that has been suggested is the adoption of a fiduciary standard that is specifically defined. Some have recommended simply applying the principles of agency law to the duties of loyalty and care (Sitkoff 2013). The duties under this proposal, sometimes referred to as a "universal standard of care," are more specifically delineated than the generally applicable fiduciary standards of loyalty and care. One of the drawbacks to the fiduciary standard is the requirement that courts continue to define its parameters. While some see the rich body of case law on interpretation as a positive aspect of expanding the fiduciary duty to broker/dealers, such reliance does not allow for the distinctive role that many broker/dealers play in terms of limited interaction with clients. The Securities Industry and Financial Markets Association (SIFMA) supports such a universal standard of care, but so do many of those who lobbied for the imposition of fiduciary duty.[40] For example, Varnavides (2011) suggests that the five core principles of the Committee for the Fiduciary Standard—established in 2009 and listed on the committee's website (http://www.thefiduciarystandard.org)—act as the components of a federal fiduciary standard:

> Put the client's best interests first;
>
> Act with prudence, that is, with the skill, care, diligence and good judgment of a professional;
>
> Do not mislead clients—provide conspicuous, full and fair disclosure of all important facts;
>
> Avoid conflicts of interest;
>
> Fully disclose and fairly manage, in the client's favor, unavoidable conflicts.[41]

These types of specific proposals—directed at the conduct that resulted in market collapse and that is the focus of both the SEC study and the emotion behind the push for reclassification of broker/dealers—are effective ways to have input into the structure of the proposed rules. Specific types of duties offer

[40]Christina Mucciolo, "Brokers versus Advisors—SIFMA Wants 'Universal,' Not Fiduciary, Standard," *WealthManagement.com* (11 March 2009).

[41]By way of full disclosure, it should be noted that the Committee for the Fiduciary Standard (a lobbying group) opposes any effort to create a new set of standards to replace the existing, well-litigated, and relatively well-defined statutory, SRO, and regulatory fiduciary standard (see www.thefiduciarystandard.org; retrieved 23 May 2014). The Committee for the Fiduciary Standard emphasizes the results of a study by Finke and Langdon (2012) that concluded that the imposition of the fiduciary standard on broker/dealers would have no impact on the ability of investors to obtain services. The Committee for the Fiduciary Standard partially funded Finke and Langdon's study.

a common ground for change without the drawbacks of the imposition of traditional fiduciary duties. Working with the opposition at the regulatory phase of the cycle is a critical part of having some input in the structure of the final rule.

Another suggestion that has been advanced is the adoption of the sole interest (or sole benefit or exclusive benefit) standard, which is a principle of trust law that requires a trustee to carry out trust duties solely in the interest of the beneficiary. Under this standard, conflicts are not permitted. However, the drawback is that this standard is ultimately dependent on judicial interpretation of "best interest." A slight modification of this standard specifies the best interest of the client, which would be predefined as being determined by a cost/benefit analysis with regard to the impact on the client (Di Lorenzo 2012). This standard has the benefit of being predefined but carries with it the increased costs of the monitoring that broker/dealers would have to undertake. As part of the "best interest" standard, there is a recommendation that mandatory arbitration in the industry be eliminated so that the courts can develop a rich body of case law on the standard. The costs of litigation and development of this new standard would be substantial.

Strengthen SROs and Enhance Enforcement. Self-regulation is a tool that can be used at any stage of the regulatory cycle, but it is most effective in the latency and awareness stages. Most broker/dealers did not engage in Goldman-type behaviors, and many investment firms offered advice to clients about risk levels and problems with the market in the lead-up to 2008. In the panic of the activism stage of the regulatory cycle, advocates often lose sight of the efforts of many within a targeted industry because of the glare from the misconduct of a few. Because regulation appears to be looming, industries often take a resistant posture during the regulatory phase. That posture is counterproductive to input. In the regulatory phase, self-regulation is needed, welcome, and reassuring. Continuing to adopt standards higher than the legal minimums is a means of negotiation during this final phase. However, adoption of higher standards is also a means of achieving both client and broker/dealer protections. In the Goldman Sachs situation, the simple adoption of a self-regulatory standard of always disclosing conflicts, a standard much higher than the loophole reliance on "But I am not a fiduciary," would have curbed the outrage over short positions against clients.

The focus in developing regulation should be on establishing clear parameters based on industry cases in which there was egregious behavior. Such over-the-top situations need to be used for shaping self-regulation. When the industry responds to the over-the-top conduct, any regulation that follows or is demanded by those who experience losses addresses what is happening that is wrong within the industry while leaving intact what the industry is doing well, and all of this activity is undertaken for the benefit of clients.

The Goldman example is not a singular bad act. For example, in 2006, the SEC filed suit against a group of broker/dealers working for World Financial Group (WFG). These broker/dealers had persuaded customers to refinance their homes through a related mortgage company (Ainsworth Mortgage). The broker/dealers then recommended that the clients use the proceeds from refinancing to purchase securities—namely, variable universal life insurance (VUL) policies.

One example given in the complaint involved the marketing director of WFG and a branch manager at Ainsworth Mortgage, who recommended that a client refinance his home with a negative amortization loan and use the proceeds to purchase VUL securities. The client was a 41-year-old truck driver who barely spoke English, had four young children, and had a combined family income of $15,000 in the year he purchased the VUL. The transaction required a $9,000 upfront payment and $500 monthly premiums thereafter. The subprime mortgage used to finance this transaction had a substantial prepayment penalty and variable interest payments. This type of case screams, "Unsuitability!" A fiduciary standard is not necessary to curb these types of broker/dealer activities. Perhaps higher penalties, faster disposition of cases, or industry recovery funds would accomplish the removal of bad actors from the industry (Di Lorenzo 2012).

Once these basic issues are addressed, the profession and regulators can move into those situations where the actions of the broker/dealer are not as blatant. For example, Di Lorenzo (2012) uses the following example as support for the use of the best interest standard for broker/dealers:

> Consider a hypothetical investor in retirement who invests solely to maintain income levels, and not for growth prospects. He is not a sophisticated investor but has been a client of a particular broker-dealer for ten years. The broker-dealer is fully informed of the investor's goals, financial situation, and other factors relevant to an informed investment recommendation. The question here turns on the quality of the broker-dealer's recommendation and not the circumstances surrounding that recommendation.
>
> In this case, there is no clear answer whether the broker-dealer acts in the client's best interest by recommending securities. A court would have to look at all of the available facts in context and ask whether the recommendation was reasonable. Was there a conflict of interest? If there was a conflict, did the conflict so govern the broker-dealer that he would make the recommendation regardless of any inquiry into the client's status? If there was no immediately ascertainable conflict, did the broker-dealer inquire into the retail client's financial situation to assess whether the recommendation is a good fit, or is the broker-dealer churning the account to generate commissions? If the recommendation is in accordance with the client's financial position, does the recommendation's potential benefit outweigh the risk of harm from investing? These are all questions that will necessarily turn on the facts of a given case. Here, the court might look more favorably, for example, on a broker-dealer who took extra time

> to educate the client on the risks of investing in a turbulent market. Consent alone should not eliminate a broker-dealer's duty to act in the client's best interest, but the circumstances surrounding consent may be evidence of the care we want broker-dealers to exercise when making a recommendation. By answering these questions in light of the purposes of the securities laws—namely investor protection and further professionalization of the securities industry—the courts will help create a robust doctrine governing the duties owed by broker-dealers to their retail clients when providing personalized investment advice. (p. 326)

The focus in analyzing such hypotheticals as this one, which is different from the blatant examples that fuel the regulatory cycle, is on returning to the underlying statutory authority and goals—investor protection, trust, and professionalism in the broker/dealer industry (Buerstetta 1996). With those goals in mind, the resolution of the hypothetical depends on *all* of the actions the broker/dealer took and whether those actions were appropriate given the nature of the client and the client's needs.

The formula is not the same for all clients. In the interest of market efficiencies, and taking into account client desires and expertise, a broker/dealer should not be treating all clients the same way in meeting this proposed best interest standard. Thinking through these types of hypotheticals helps illuminate the idea that broad policies that impose a single standard may not bring the protection that such sweeping regulations are intended to deliver. Such hypotheticals as this one can offer insight into how regulation should be shaped to provide for the protection of investors while advancing the professionalism of broker/dealers.

Conclusion

As financial professions and industries undertake additional self-regulation, those involved should understand that the purpose of self-regulation is not to determine, "What can I get away with under the law?" Rather, its purpose is to provide investors with a picture of investment professionals: This is who we are, this is what we do, and this is what we will not do. If those components are not present because of weak existing SRO standards or inadequate enforcement, then the focus during this seemingly final part of the regulatory cycle should be not only on the proposed regulations but also on the contemplation of higher standards. In addition, incorporating rigor into existing standards and into the organization's enforcement proceedings helps to define or, if necessary, redefine the industry's ethical commitment. A candid evaluation of industry conduct, discipline, and rules is necessary to earn credibility during any phase of the regulatory cycle.

This qualifies for 1 CE credit, inclusive of 1 SER credit.

Bibliography

Angel, James J., and Douglas McCabe. 2013. "Ethical Standards for Stockbrokers: Fiduciary or Suitability?" *Journal of Business Ethics*, vol. 115, no. 1 (June):183–193.

The authors argue that the standard of recommending "suitable" investments to clients is too weak. They discuss current proposals to raise the standard to a fiduciary one, a standard that would require recommendations that are in the best interest of the clients. The authors compare investment advisers with doctors and auto mechanics, whose product consists of both the professional advice and the implementation. Conflicts of interest, including the availability of higher commissions for the adviser's employer's products, require disclosure, and recommendations should be based on the client's best interest, not on returns for the adviser. Interestingly, the authors also recognize the role of advisers in providing capital for investments: Financial markets thrive when financial products are distributed, and ongoing distributions benefit many, including the clients. The authors conclude that some conflicts of interest, such as those that spring from commissions, may be tolerable in the interest of progress in the financial markets. However, the key to fulfilling fiduciary responsibility is disclosure.

Arnott, Robert D. 2006. "The Fiduciary Time Line: Implications for Asset Allocation." *Financial Analysts Journal*, vol. 62, no. 2 (March/April):8–10.

The author documents the distinctly different perspectives of the fiduciary agent (investment adviser) and the client. "The fiduciary's time line, which is measured in decades, differs starkly from the agent's time line, which is measured in years" (p. 8). And a review of returns over these differing lengths of time results in this conclusion: "Those who say that we must be willing to take risks to earn lofty returns are clearly correct. But those who say that a willingness to take risk will deliver high returns are just as clearly wrong. The high-risk markets are clustered toward the top *and bottom* of the distribution" (p. 10).

Bai, Lynn. 2014. "Broker-Dealers, Institutional Investors, and Fiduciary Duty: Much Ado about Nothing?" *William and Mary Business Law Review*, vol. 5, no. 1:55–104.

This article focuses on the advisability of imposing a fiduciary duty on broker/dealers for institutional investors. A fiduciary duty could potentially enhance broker/dealers' standard of conduct only for a subset of institutional investors who are well capitalized, are capable of assessing risks independently, and acknowledge in writing their nonreliance on broker/dealers' advice. Thus, the benefit of fiduciary duty is much narrower than its proponents believe. In addition, institutional investors face substantial obstacles in recovering damages from broker/dealers who violate their standard of conduct through private litigation, and yet fiduciary duty would not help in this regard. In light of fiduciary duty's negligible benefit and indeterminate cost to the financial industry, the piece concludes that it is not a viable measure for enhancing institutional investor protection.

Ben-Shahar, Omri, and Carl E. Schneider. 2011. "The Failure of Mandated Disclosure." *University of Pennsylvania Law Review*, vol. 159, no. 3:647–749.

While the article covers several professions and types of mandatory disclosure, its general conclusion for all forms of disclosure, from conflicts of interest to material information in credit transactions, is that, for a multitude of reasons, mandated disclosures fail. The reasons for the failure of mandatory disclosures include the political dynamics underlying the enactment of these mandates, the incentives of disclosers to carry them out, and the ability of disclosees (users) to use them. The piece argues that mandated disclosures not only fail to achieve their stated goals but also lead to unintended consequences that often harm the very people the disclosures are intended to serve. For example, one of the critical points the author makes is that the presence of mandatory information tends to give users a false sense of confidence that results in their failure to ask questions of friends, family, and others with experience in a particular area about a product, a service, or promises of performance. The authors note the success of such services as eBay and Angie's List, where purchasers buy from unknown sellers and service providers on the basis of information that they gather themselves from other users, whose posts are available in one convenient location. The authors believe that these types of forums are more effective than mandatory disclosure requirements.

Buerstetta, Grant E. 1996. "Creating a Flexible Fiduciary Duty Rule for Banks Entering into Proprietary Derivatives Contracts." *Annual Review of Banking*, vol. 15:395–431.

This piece illustrates one of the many waves of regulatory reform proposed following market collapses and resulting significant investor losses. It was written following the bankruptcy of Orange County, California, which resulted from the significant investments made by its treasurer in derivatives, as well as in such companies as Gibson Greetings (the types of holdings not generally deemed to carry high risk). The author proposes a form of flexible fiduciary duty for broker/dealers that would demand a higher level of client education and/or disclosure when the types of investments recommended carry complexities as well as higher risk. Although the piece is directed at banks' roles with clients, its recommendations are generally applicable to investment professionals. The author's focus is on a sense of fairness on the part of the investment professional in terms of disclosure with clients.

Coffee, John C., Jr. 2004. "Gatekeeper Failure and Reform: The Challenge of Fashioning Relevant Reforms." *Boston University Law Review*, vol. 84, no. 2 (April):302–303.

Professor Coffee argues that analysts are gatekeepers of information (similar to auditors and attorneys for corporations) and that, as gatekeepers, they have a responsibility to ensure accurate information and should be subject to the following regulatory reforms: (1) structural rules, which, for example, subject gatekeepers to greater public oversight; (2) prophylactic rules, which typically seek to preclude conflicts of interest; (3) "empowerment" rules, which seek to ensure greater independence or to give the gatekeeper greater leverage over the principal that it is expected to monitor; and (4) liability-enhancing rules.

DeMott, Deborah A. 2013. "The Crucial but (Potentially) Precarious Position of the Chief Compliance Officer." *Brooklyn Journal of Corporate, Financial & Commercial Law*, vol. 8, no. 1 (Fall):56–79.

This article addresses the issues of broker/dealer relationships with clients from the perspective of firm compliance and includes a discussion of regulatory failures to curb abuses. The author examines a series of recent cases to illustrate that legal doctrine and regulation may sometimes undermine the effectiveness of compliance systems and personnel, as opposed to enhancing a firm's incentives to strengthen internal compliance systems and the positions of those who staff them. The author concludes that the relationship between a firm's reputation and the quality of its internal compliance personnel and systems is critical and should be a focus of self-reform.

Di Lorenzo, Nicholas S. 2012. "Defining a New Punctilio of an Honor: The Best Interest Standard for Broker-Dealers." *Boston University Law Review*, vol. 92:291–327.

The author argues that the mere imposition of a heightened fiduciary duty is unlikely to foster the change that Dodd–Frank was intended to produce. As interpreted by the SEC, the Investment Advisers Act of 1940 currently requires investment advisers to act in their clients' best interest. Although defined by certain requirements, this standard is vague. The author offers a two-part proposal that will help support the development of a robust best interest standard. First, the best interest standard as applied to broker/dealers should be based on analogous trust law concepts and not on the current best interest standard applicable to investment advisers. Second, the SEC should exercise its authority under Dodd–Frank to eliminate mandatory arbitration agreements in client contracts to support the transparency necessary to develop a robust doctrine. The author believes that these suggestions would not only accomplish the policy goals of Dodd–Frank by reducing the potential for conflicts of interest between investment professionals and their clients but would also be less cost prohibitive and more practical than other alternatives.

Droms, William G. 1992. "Fiduciary Responsibilities of Investment Managers and Trustees." *Financial Analysts Journal*, vol. 48, no. 4 (July/August):58–64.

This piece is historical, taking us from the 1970s through the early 1990s, including a look at federal legislative changes. The article covers fiduciary responsibilities found in case law, Scott's *Law of Trusts*, the American Law Institute's *Restatement (Second) of Trusts*, the Uniform Management of Institutional Funds Act of 1972 (UMIFA), and Section 4944 of the Internal Revenue Code, as well as the peculiar duties outlined in the Employee Retirement Income Security Act of 1974 (ERISA). The article breaks down fiduciary responsibilities into two generic categories: the duty of undivided loyalty (conflicts) and the standard of reasonable care (prudence). The piece also ties portfolio management theory into the duty of prudence.

Easterbrook, Frank H., and Daniel R. Fischel. 1993. "Contract and Fiduciary Duty." *Journal of Law and Economics*, vol. 36, no. 1 (April):425–446.

The authors argue that fiduciary duties are actually contractual relationship issues that the parties should resolve among themselves. They also argue that acting on moral beliefs (i.e., the imposition of a general professional or statutory fiduciary duty standard) will not make investors better off but will instead lead to fewer broker/dealers and advisers or higher costs for hiring broker/dealers and advisers. The imposition of the vague notion of "fiduciary duty" fails to take into consideration the economic issues in relationships that vary significantly, according to the authors. Their resolution is the use of economic considerations as sound footing for determining the need for or scope of fiduciary duties. "Managers owe fiduciary duties to equity investors, but not debt investors or employees, because these claimants can contract at low cost, while the costs of specification are prohibitively high for the residual claimants. A trustee is held to the strict 'prudent man' standard, while a partner is not, because the trustee can diversify across investments at low cost and so protect the beneficiary, while partners typically specialize and accept additional risk, partners having more in common with managers and equity investors than with orphans and charitable institutions. Managers and partners may undertake some self-interested transactions in order to encourage (by allowing reward) the process of finding new opportunities for effectively risk-neutral firms. The strict ban on self-interested transactions for trustees prevents this activity and achieves the benefit of passive diversification for risk-averse beneficiaries. The law of trusts thus discourages what the law of corporations encourages—and in each case all parties are better off" (p. 437).

Finke, Michael, and Thomas Langdon. 2012. "The Impact of the Broker-Dealer Fiduciary Standard on Financial Advice." *Journal of Financial Planning*, vol. 25, no. 7 (July):28–37.

The authors conducted a study of the imposition on broker/dealers of a stricter legal fiduciary standard by asking broker/dealers a series of questions about their relationships with clients and comparing the responses of broker/dealers in states where such a fiduciary duty is already imposed with those of broker/dealers in states where such a fiduciary duty is not imposed. The authors conclude that there is "no evidence that the broker-dealer industry is affected significantly by the imposition of a stricter legal fiduciary standard on the conduct of registered representatives" (p. 36). The authors add that the opposition of the industry to the application of stricter regulations suggests that the agency costs that exist when brokers are regulated according to suitability are significant. However, they conclude that there is a net welfare gain to society and that broker/dealers are likely to continue to operate in the same way they have under current standards.

Fisch, Jill E. 2006. "Fiduciary Duties and the Analyst Scandals." *Alabama Law Review*, vol. 58, no. 5:1083–1102.

The published text of a lecture given by Professor Fisch, this piece documents the analyst scandals from the 1990s through 2006 (just prior to the 2008 market collapse). The focus of the piece is on research analysts and the conflicts they routinely face because their employers both provide research and engage in securities transactions. The author is not terribly troubled by the dual role of analysts because, as she concludes, analysts may be overly optimistic in their research, but they are also correct more often than they are wrong.

Gillis, John G. 1972. "Securities Law and Regulation: Professional Fiduciaries under Fire." *Financial Analysts Journal*, vol. 28, no. 5 (September/October):10, 14–15, 87–89.

The author documents the uptick (in 1972) of attacks against the managers of mutual funds as fiduciaries. Interestingly, he attributes the uptick to increased availability of information about securities and their performance, the volatility of the securities markets, the greater availability of class actions, the growth of theories of legal recovery, and an increasingly litigious society. These causes have not disappeared, and neither has the discussion of fiduciary responsibilities. The cases discussed involve conflicts of interest that were not managed properly by the investment advisers. Recommendations for reform include annual full disclosure to investors about dealings of the adviser, loans made from the fund, and larger investments (over $100,000) of the fund. The author also recommends fines for violations of the duty to disclose.

Gillis, John G., and William F. Weld. 1972. "Securities Law and Regulation: The Money Manager as Fiduciary." *Financial Analysts Journal*, vol. 28, no. 2 (March/April):10, 12, 14, 92–93.

The article, which was one of the first to deal with conflicts and fiduciary duty, serves to document that not much has changed since 1972, when this piece was published. The article begins with a summary of court decisions on money managers, which includes an example in which a money manager was churning to earn commissions and was benefiting from stock trades in which it represented both buyer and seller. The article focuses on a suggestion that would become part of the 2013 literature—namely, that the application of common law agency principles should govern in these situations and should be used to determine liability.

Hurt, Christine. 2014. "The Duty to Manage Risk." *Journal of Corporation Law*, vol. 39, no. 2 (Winter):253–293.

This analysis from the perspective of corporate fiduciary duty offers a look at the legal and ethical issues involved in managing risk, including the imposition of liability for exposing shareholders to excessive risk. Using the backdrop of the 2008 market collapse, the piece examines whether there should be liability for exposing investors to excessive risk. It includes an excellent summary of the case law on liability when investors claim something other than securities fraud, providing a handy overview of where we have been and where we are on fiduciary duty and liability for something less than fraud. However, the analysis is also forward looking in its discussion of duty of care, duty of loyalty, and duty of oversight to shareholders and clients and whether these standards should be changed to impose liability for generic and undisclosed risk. The piece offers the following observation about the distinctions among criminal liability, civil liability, and foolishness with others' money:

"What has understandably angered the investing community, workers, and homeowners in the wake of the financial crisis has been the otherwise-legal risk taking climates at financial firms that encouraged traders and other employees to use firm assets to take risky investment positions—originating, holding, or purchasing residential mortgage-backed securities (RMBS); selling credit default swaps (CDS) related to RMBS; purchasing or selling collateralized debt obligations (CDOs) related to RMBS; or some combination thereof. Continuing to invest, even heavily, in these types of securities in the face of negative financial forecasts was not illegal, nor was being highly leveraged. Unfortunately, state and federal laws are not good at criminalizing foolishness, even foolishness involving other people's money" (p. 257).

The article also notes that courts have steered clear, and rightly so, of imposing liability on such organizations as Goldman Sachs for putting compensation plans in place that gave rise to gross negligence and waste at the firm. Again, incentives that lead folks down risky paths do not constitute culpable gross negligence for purposes of investor recovery.

The article concludes that the imposition of fiduciary duty on corporations and investment firms would create liability using hindsight's perspective, thereby removing the responsibility for determining risk levels from individual investors, something that would require substituting judicial review for investor caution.

Jennings, Marianne M. 1992. "The Cycle of Litigation Crises: Foreseeable but Not Foreseen." *Preventive Law Reporter*, vol. 11, no. 3 (September):7–11.

Based on the work of political scientist James Frierson, this article discusses how issues progress from being ethical dilemmas to evolving abuses that result in emotional public reactions and regulation. A voluntary fix is no longer an option when an industry becomes the target of emotional actions and testimony by those who were harmed by poor ethical choices within the industry.

———. 2006. "How Ethics Trumps Market Inefficiencies and Thwarts the Need for Regulation." *Corporate Finance Review*, vol. 10, no. 5:36–41.

Applying the regulatory cycle to the financial industry, this article shows how the failure of voluntary action in the financial markets resulted in regulation that introduced systemic costs and exacerbated the issues it was designed to address.

Lin, Tom C.W. 2014. "The New Financial Industry." *Alabama Law Review*, vol. 65, no. 3:567–623.

The author provides an excellent historical perspective on the financial markets as well as a forward-looking analysis of future regulation. This article is one of the few that acknowledge changing dynamics in the financial markets as well as in investors. A financial industry once dominated by humans has evolved into one where humans and machines share power. Modern finance is becoming cyborg finance—an industry that is faster, larger, more complex, more global, more interconnected, and less human.

This article offers an early systemic examination of this ongoing financial transformation and proposes new guiding principles for the future of financial regulation. Drawing from a rich literature on past financial crises and transformations, the article explores the next big movement in finance and financial regulation and offers fresh insights for better addressing the perils and promises emerging from the new financial industry.

Lydenberg, Steve. 2014. "Reason, Rationality, and Fiduciary Duty." *Journal of Business Ethics*, vol. 119, no. 3 (February):365–380.

In this perspective piece, the author argues that for the last two decades, modern finance has directed fiduciaries to act "rationally," or in the sole financial interest of their funds or clients, thereby downplaying the effects of their investments on others. The author presents a history of fiduciaries in prior decades and concludes that wisdom, discretion, and intelligence were a part of the fiduciaries' approach, including the effects of their investment decisions on others and the world. The piece argues for investment decisions that acknowledge fiduciary duties to present and future generations. The author concludes that part of the adviser's fiduciary duty is to realize the full potential of the investment assets entrusted to the adviser's care by balancing long-term and short-term gains.

Prentice, Robert A. 2011. "Moral Equilibrium: Stock Brokers and the Limits of Disclosure." *Wisconsin Law Review*, vol. 2011, no. 6:1059–1107.

Written during the period of SEC rule making under Dodd–Frank, which required that some rules be developed for broker disclosures to clients, the piece narrows the analysis of mandatory disclosure to brokers and also applies principles of behavioral psychology and new developments in behavioral ethics to argue for different forms of disclosure (beyond regulatory proposals at the time) that could be more helpful to users and contribute to the restoration of market trust and financial market stability.

Rogers, John. 2014. "A New Era of Fiduciary Capitalism? Let's Hope So." *Financial Analysts Journal*, vol. 70, no. 3 (May/June):6–12.

The author offers an interesting perspective on the distinction between financial capitalism and fiduciary capitalism. The essay proposes a shift to fiduciary capitalism, a market system in which we come to acknowledge the distinction between the needs, knowledge, and expectations of institutional investors and the same traits in investors who deal with financial intermediaries. The secrecy of institutional investors is almost antithetical to the demands of fiduciary duty. The investment professionals who will succeed in fiduciary capitalism are those who are able to determine the needs of various types of investors and step in to meet those needs. New compensation models, new types of services, and new respect for retail investors will be factors in this refocused market system.

Romano, Roberta. 1993. "Comment on Easterbrook and Fischel, 'Contract and Fiduciary Duty.'" *Journal of Law and Economics*, vol. 36, no. 1 (April):447–451.

Professor Romano agrees with Easterbrook and Fischel on the following points: (1) Economics has something useful to offer in analyzing fiduciary duties, (2) fiduciary duties can be best understood from a contractual approach, (3) the contractual approach is helpful even though some courts do not use the language of contracts when analyzing fiduciary duties, (4) parties will adjust to (contract around) judicial opinions imposing unwanted fiduciary duties, and (5) noneconomic theories do not successfully explain the doctrine.

However, she finds their claim that fiduciary duty is not a distinctive relationship to be problematic. She concludes that the reason for the imposition of fiduciary duties in certain circumstances is that there is something especially difficult about contract specifications and monitoring costs that requires that special duties be imposed. She uses the example of ERISA, the nature of the long-term relationships thereunder, and the difficulty beneficiaries have computing what they will need for retirement and how they can get to that point through contributions and investment. The distinctive nature of the relationships explains the economic need for the imposition of fiduciary standards.

Schwarcz, Steven L. 2005. "Temporal Perspectives: Resolving the Conflicts Between Current and Future Investors." *Minnesota Law Review*, vol. 89:1044–1091.

Professor Schwarcz argues that there are inherently conflicted players in the financial markets. The fundamental goal of securities law is to make markets more efficient by providing transparency to investors, thereby reducing asymmetric information. The fundamental goal of corporation law is to cause managers to govern for the benefit of the firm and its investors. The fundamental goal of credit-rating agencies is to provide ratings that accurately inform investors of the likelihood of timely payment on a firm's bonds. The result is that the investor audience within each of these areas of law is confused. An understanding of the temporal conflict also reveals that widespread perceptions of corporate wrongdoing can be misleading when corporate actions taken *ex ante* to benefit one investor group inadvertently harm another investor group *ex post*.

The article then proposes resolving the inherent conflict by analyzing, in each case, who should be included in the relevant audience.

Sitkoff, Robert H. 2013. "The Fiduciary Obligations of Financial Advisors Under the Law of Agency." Harvard Public Law Working Paper No. 13-16.

Professor Sitkoff takes a different approach to the issue of fiduciary duty by concluding that whether a financial professional is a broker, an adviser, or an analyst, that professional is still working for and on behalf of another and is, therefore, an agent under common law and thereby subject to the standards of a fiduciary, including the duty of loyalty. He advocates holding advisers liable for any breach of that common law agency fiduciary duty.

Interestingly, Professor Sitkoff includes a disclaimer at the beginning of his paper that indicates that he works with professionals in the financial markets who may or may not have an interest in seeing that his views become part of the market's self-governance.

Slaughter, Stacey P. 2014. "Advising Clients in a Changing Securities Law Environment." In *New Developments in Securities Litigation*. New York: Thomson Reuters/Aspatore.

Written from the perspective of a litigation specialist, this article offers practical tips for investment advisers, as well as brokers and dealers, for effective client relationships. The article also provides an excellent summary of the regulatory structure for advisers and broker/dealers in the financial markets.

Strier, Franklin. 2005. "How Our Fiduciary Institutions Have Betrayed Our Trust." *Journal of Legal, Ethical and Regulatory Issues*, vol. 8, no. 2:45–69.

As one of the first post-Enron articles on fiduciary duty, this piece provides a review of the resulting legislative changes, as well as information about the public loss of trust.

Part I assesses the loss of trust in financial institutions among investors and the general public, as measured by various surveys. Part II reviews the specific transgressions by the trusted institutions that aroused the investing public's sense of betrayal. Part III is a legislative summary and a review of proposed legal reforms designed to prevent further erosion of trust. Knowing the outcome, the reader will find irony in the hopeful reforms section.

Varnavides, Gary A. 2011. "The Flawed State of Broker-Dealer Regulation and the Case for an Authentic Federal Fiduciary Standard for Broker-Dealers." *Fordham Journal of Corporate & Financial Law*, vol. 16, no. 1:203–225.

The 2008 financial crisis revealed that the US financial industry's regulatory scheme is broken and in desperate need of reform. The modern US financial system operates under an antiquated regulatory structure developed in the 1930s and 1940s that is ill equipped to deal with the intricacies and risks of modern finance. This piece addresses a critical section of the Investor Protection Act of 2009 (IPA): its proposal that broker/dealers be held to a new, higher standard of conduct toward customers modeled on the Investment Advisers Act of 1940. Part II of this article discusses the history of broker/dealer and investment adviser regulation, including the development of different legal duties and regulatory schemes for each group. Part III identifies and analyzes the different contexts in which broker/dealers and investment advisers are held to a fiduciary standard. Part IV examines the central problems within the current regulatory framework for broker/dealers and investment advisers.

Walsh, Paul R., and David W. Johns. 2013. "Can the Retail Investor Survive the Fiduciary Standard?" *St. John's Law Review*, vol. 87, no. 2 (Spring–Summer):437–449.

For the retail investor in the United States seeking professional investment advice, two options are generally available: broker/dealers and investment advisers. The two entities are governed under separate regulatory schemes. With the recent financial collapse and the ensuing jump to regulation, there is a push to establish a uniform standard for all investment recommendations—a fiduciary standard—that would be a one-size-fits-all reaction, leading to less access and higher costs for the smaller investor. Continued regulation of more disclosure and transparency in the investment sales process, stronger requirements of the investment salesperson, proliferation of common-sense education of the investing public in handling their own money, and swifter punishment of bad actors under existing rules should be the regulatory focus.

Wrona, James S. 2012. "The Best of Both Worlds: A Fact-Based Analysis of the Legal Obligations of Investment Advisers and Broker-Dealers and a Framework for Enhanced Investor Protection." *Business Lawyer*, vol. 68, no. 1 (November):1–56.

A crucial debate on financial regulatory reform, affecting virtually every investor in the United States, is now taking place. The debate centers on the standards of care required of financial professionals when they provide investment advice. Two separate and markedly different regulatory regimes apply to these financial professionals: one for investment advisers and another for broker/dealers. This article discusses recent congressional initiatives related to advisers and broker/dealers, reviews existing obligations when advisers and broker/dealers provide advice to customers, and identifies regulatory gaps that need to be bridged. The level of regulatory oversight that both models receive is also explored. Finally, the article offers a framework to ensure robust investor protection and, as part of that framework, recommends that policymakers impose additional obligations on both broker/dealers and advisers to achieve truly universal standards of conduct that are in investors' best interest.

Made in the USA
Monee, IL
04 January 2025

76041370R00024